SOUTH KOREA TOURIST GUIDE 2023: A Comprehensive Travel Guide

Elizabeth Nicoll

INTRODUCTION

I was always fascinated by the rich culture, history, and technology of South Korea, so when the opportunity finally presented itself, I eagerly embarked on a journey to explore the country.

As soon as I arrived in Seoul, I was in awe of the city's bustling energy. Towering skyscrapers, intricate temples, and bustling street markets left me spellbound. Every day was filled with new experiences, from trying delicious Korean cuisine to exploring historic palaces.
One of my most memorable moments was visiting Jeju Island. The stunning natural beauty and serene landscapes took my breath away, and I was able to witness the traditional culture of the island, including the famous haenyeo female divers.
After two weeks of unforgettable experiences, I realized that planning a trip to such a diverse and exciting country could be overwhelming for some. That's why I decided to share my

experiences and insights to make it easier for others to plan their own trip to South Korea.
I put together a comprehensive guide that covers everything from where to stay and what to see, to what to eat and how to get around. I included tips and recommendations based on my own experiences to make the journey as smooth and enjoyable as possible.

Now, it's your turn. Use my guide to plan your own unforgettable journey to South Korea. And who knows, maybe one day you too will be inspired to share your experiences with others.

INTRODUCTION

CHAPTER 1
OVERVIEW OF SOUTH KOREA
WHAT TO DO IN SOUTH KOREA

CHAPTER 2 BEST TIME TO VISIT
Tourist Attractions in South Korea
Festivals And Events In South Korea
Best Times And Locations To See Cherry Blossom
The Best Time To Visit For The Seoul Lotus Lantern Festival

CHAPTER 3: PLACES TO VISIT IN SOUTH KOREA
Places To Visit In Incheon
Places To Visit In JEJU
Locations To See In BUSAN

DESTINATIONS IN SOUTH KOREA THAT IS BEST FOR
SOLO TRAVELLERS

CHAPTER 4 BANK CARDS AND CURRENCY
The Best Accepted South Korea Bank Cards
Best Locations In South Korea To Change Currencies To
WON

CHAPTER 5 K-ETA
A List Of Nations That Have K-ETA
Exceptions For Submitting An Application For The K-ETA
K-ETA Application Procedure
Requirements For The K-ETA
Validity Term
Fees For The K-ETA
Reapplication
Complete Travel Advice

local laws

CHAPTER 6: THINGS YOU SHOULD KNOW
Informations Visitors Need To Know
Entry Procedures For Foreign Visitors
Rules To Follow as a Tourist or Foreigner

CHAPTER 7: TRANSPORTATION
Transportation in South korea
The Easiest Form Of Transportation In Sour Korea
THE KAKOA TAXI
The Usual Method of Paying Kokao Taxi
The Difference Between the Blue and General Taxis
South Korea's KTX Train
Requirements for Obtaining a KTX Train Ticket
The Difference Between a KTX First-Class Ticket and a
Standard-Class Ticket
PROCESS OF BOOKING A FERRY

Tips for Traveling With Infants to South Korea
Selecting Flights
Being Comfortable
Entertainment during flying
Food choices
creating a backup strategy for the aircraft

ACCOMMODATION ARRANGEMENTS IN SOUTH KOREA
Good Hotels In Myeongdong
Good Hotels In JEJU
Good Hotels In Busan
Good Hotels In Incheon
Good Hotels In Hongdae

CHAPTER 8:

SOUTH KOREA'S FOOD AND DRINK
FANTASTIC RESTAURANTS IN SEOUL

CHAPTER 9
SOUTH KOREA'S HEALTH AND SAFETY
Safety Precautions:
Health Considerations:
Emergency Contact Numbers:
SCAM ALERTS

CHAPTER 10 BEST KOREA SIM CARD FOR TRAVELERS
IN 2023
List of Applications you'll Need When Traveling in South
Korea
ROAMING
The Best Tourist SIM For Longer Stays
What to look for and Consider When Purchasing a Korean
Travel SIM
How to Examine a South Korean SIM card Before purchasing
one
Duration
Allowance for data
Take up
various-size SIM
The Benefits of Placing an Advance Purchase for Your
Korean SIM card
CONCLUSION

CHAPTER 1

OVERVIEW OF SOUTH KOREA

South Korea, sometimes referred to as the Republic of Korea, is a nation on the Korean Peninsula in East Asia. Seoul, the nation's capital, is home to more than 51 million people. South Korea is a developed economic powerhouse with cutting-edge technology, a rich cultural history, and a high level of life. The nation is home to a distinctive mix of contemporary cities and old buildings, as well as historical sites, picturesque mountains, beaches, and cultural events. In addition, South Korea is renowned for its contributions to a number of sectors, including fashion, technology, and transportation, as well as for its delectable food, which includes delicacies like bibimbap, bulgogi, and kimchi. Millions of tourists travel there each year, making it a well-known tourist attraction.

WHAT TO DO IN SOUTH KOREA

South Korea has a fascinating past and a rich cultural legacy, which are represented in the country's historic palaces, temples, and fortifications. Visitors may take part in customary celebrations like the Boryeong Mud Festival and the Pusan International Film Festival and discover the nation's distinctive way of life by visiting its cultural institutions, galleries, and museums.

South Korea has some of the most stunning natural vistas in the whole globe. Visitors may stroll through lush woods, discover picturesque mountain ranges, and unwind on peaceful beaches. A peaceful and refreshing experience may be had at the nation's hot springs, which are another reason for its fame.

Modern Attractions: South Korea, a nation with a booming economy and cutting-edge technology, is home to a variety of contemporary attractions in major cities. Modern technology is available for visitors to explore, along with shopping, entertainment, and some of the biggest amusement parks on the planet.

South Korean food is delectable, savory, and nutritious. Both traditional fare including bibimbap, bulgogi, and kimchi as well as a variety of foreign food are available to visitors. The nation is also home to a large number of street food stands that provide a distinctive and delectable eating experience.

CHAPTER 2 BEST TIME TO VISIT

What a traveler wishes to experience will determine the ideal time to go to South Korea. Spring (March to May) and fall (September to November) are the finest times to see the country's picturesque splendor since the weather is pleasant and the countryside is at its prettiest. For those who wish to enjoy the beaches, the summer (June to August) is also an excellent season to go, but be ready for hot and muggy conditions. For those who wish to enjoy the nation's ski resorts and winter activities, the winter (December to February) is perfect, but be ready for chilly, snowy weather.

Tourist Attractions in South Korea

Historical and Cultural Attractions: South Korea is home to a wide variety of historical and cultural sites that are open to tourists to explore. The historic city of Gyeongju, Gyeongbokgung Palace and the nearby Gwanghwamun Plaza in Seoul, and the Hwaseong Fortress in Suwon are a few of the most well-known locations. For further information on the history and culture of South Korea, visitors can also stop by the National Museum of Korea and the National Palace Museum of Korea.

South Korea is home to a plethora of natural beauty, including breathtaking landscapes, picturesque parks, and picturesque coastline regions. Jeju Island, Seoraksan National Park, and the Baekdudaegan Mountain Range are some of Korea's best-known natural attractions. To experience the verdant scenery and abundant foliage, visitors could also explore Namsan Park and Bukhansan National Park.

C. Adventure Activities: South Korea has several thrilling activities available for people seeking adventure. Rafting, hiking, mountain climbing, and winter activities like skiing and snowboarding are all available to visitors. For a genuinely thrilling experience, adventurers may also try bungee jumping, zip lining, and paragliding.

D. Shopping and entertainment: There are many places to shop in South Korea, from traditional marketplaces to cutting-edge malls. Popular shopping locations include the crowded streets of Seoul's Myeong-dong, the age-old Insadong market, and the enormous COEX Mall. Visitors may also spend the evening at one of the many entertainment venues, including theaters, music halls, and movie theaters, or they can see a traditional Korean performance like a samulnori drumming display.

Festivals And Events In South Korea

South Korea celebrates a number of national holidays throughout the year with anything from parades to fireworks. New Year's Day, Independence Day, and National Foundation Day are a few of the most significant occasions. Visitors should also be aware that Chuseok, or the Korean Thanksgiving, and the Lunar New Year, both known as Seollal, are significant holidays in South Korea that are observed with family reunions, regional cuisine, and other celebrations.

B. Cultural Festivals: The many cultural festivals held in South Korea serve to highlight the nation's rich customs, history, and cultural heritage. The Pusan International Film Festival, the Jinju Namgang Yudeung Festival, and the Boryeong Mud Festival are a few of the most well-known events. Also worth checking out are the Buyeo Seodong Lotus Festival, the Andong International Mask Dance Festival, and the Seoul Lantern Festival.

C. Religious Celebrations: Because of South Korea's extensive religious history, travelers may take in a wide range of religious events all year long. The Confucian ceremony of Charye, the Catholic procession of the Holy Cross, and the Buddhist lantern festival are a few of the most significant events. Visitors should also check out the gut ceremony, which is done by traditional Korean shamans to honor the dead and seek their blessings.

Best Times And Locations To See Cherry Blossom

There are several locations that provide breathtaking views of the pink and white flowers in South Korea, a well-known destination for cherry blossom watching. Here are some of the finest locations and times to visit South Korea to observe cherry blossoms:

Yeouido Park: Yeouido Park is a well-known location for cherry blossom viewing in Seoul. It has more than 1,000 cherry trees surrounding the Han River's banks. The best time to visit is from late March to early April.

The Jinhae Gunhangje Festival, which takes place in Jinhae on South Korea's southern coast, is known for its large cherry blossom display as well as its street food vendors, live music, and traditional Korean entertainment. Early April is when the celebration is held.

Gyeongju Cherry Blossom Event: Held in Gyeongju, South Korea's southeast, this festival is known for its stunning display of cherry blossoms around Bomun Lake. Late April is when the celebration is held.

Seokchon Lake: With more than 600 cherry trees around the lake, Seokchon Lake is a well-known location for cherry blossom watching in Seoul. Late March to early April is the ideal time to travel.

Wolyeonggyo Bridge: With more than 1,400 cherry trees bordering the banks of the Nakdong River, this bridge in Daegu is well-known for its cherry blossom displays. Late March to early April is the ideal time to travel.

Prior to making travel plans, tourists should examine the local weather prediction and cherry blossom bloom status since the precise date of the blooms might change based on the local temperature and weather.

In advance: In order to prevent disappointment during cherry blossom season, it is a good idea to plan ahead and reserve lodging, transportation, and activities well in advance.

Pay attention to crowded times: The cherry blossom season is also a busy period for local transportation and well-liked tourist locations, so tourists should be ready for crowds and organize their schedule appropriately.

Get up early: Think about waking up early in the morning and visiting before the people come to escape the crowds and take in the tranquility and beauty of the cherry blossom blooming.

Don't forget your camera; cherry blossom season only occurs once a year, so photographing the splendor of the blossoms will help you remember the trip.

Respect the environment: Visitors should be aware of their environmental effect and show respect for the cherry blossom trees and other natural surroundings by avoiding climbing them, leaving trash behind, or doing anything else to harm the ecosystem.

These pointers might help tourists get the most out of their time watching cherry blossoms in South Korea and preserve special memories of this lovely time of year.

The Best Time To Visit For The Seoul Lotus Lantern Festival

In the center of Seoul, South Korea, there is an annual celebration called the Seoul Lotus

Lantern Festival. The event, which honors Buddhist culture, includes a vibrant display of lanterns in all sizes and forms, from modest paper lanterns to enormous, ornate constructions. Both residents and visitors go to the festival, which is a terrific way to see South Korea's diverse culture and customs.

Usually around late April or early May, when the event is in full flow, is the ideal time to attend the Seoul Lotus Lantern Festival. Visitors may take part in a number of events and activities throughout the festival, including workshops for manufacturing lanterns, traditional Korean performances, and a lantern procession through Seoul's streets.

Due to its popularity and potential for crowds, visitors are advised to make travel arrangements in advance for the festival. It's a smart idea to make travel and lodging arrangements in advance, as well as to review the festival calendar for any particular events or activities you may be interested in.

Anyone interested in learning more about the fascinating customs and history of South Korea should definitely attend the Seoul Lotus Lantern Festival, which is a distinctive and colorful celebration of South Korean culture.

CHAPTER 3: PLACES TO VISIT IN SOUTH KOREA

There are several locations to explore and activities to engage in in South Korea, a nation with a rich cultural legacy and stunning natural surroundings.

Here is a list of some of South Korea's top tourist destinations:

Jeju Island is a well-liked holiday spot, renowned for the visual magnificence of its beaches, waterfalls, and volcanic scenery.

Namsan Tower is a Seoul landmark that provides panoramic city views and is a well-liked location for romantic occasions.

A mountainous national park on South Korea's east coast, Seoraksan is renowned for its picturesque splendor, which includes magnificent autumn foliage.

Busan is a coastal city in South Korea that's known for its seafood, beaches, and annual film festival.

The Demilitarized Zone (DMZ), a sliver of territory between North and South Korea, provides a unique perspective on the history and warfare between the two nations.

Suwon's Hwaseong Fortress, a UNESCO World Heritage site and a prime example of traditional Korean military architecture, was built in the 18th century.

Insadong A district in the heart of Seoul noted for its traditional tea houses, antique stores, and traditional Korean arts and crafts.

Jogyesa Temple: One of the biggest and most significant Buddhist temples in South Korea, which is a Buddhist temple in the heart of Seoul.

Jeonju Hanok Town is a well-preserved traditional Korean village that is well-known for both its regional food and its well-preserved traditional Korean homes, or "hanok."

Busan's Haeundae Beach is a well-liked beach with crystal-clear waves and smooth sand.

Seongsan Ilchulbong, a volcanic tuff cone on Jeju Island that is a UNESCO World Heritage site, is renowned for its visual splendor and hiking paths.

Changdeokgung Palace, a historic royal residence in the heart of Seoul, is renowned for its exquisite grounds and well-preserved ancient architecture.

Gamcheon Culture Village is a district in Busan distinguished by its vividly painted homes, street art, and independent stores and eateries.

Places To Visit In Incheon

These are some of the well-liked tourism attractions in Incheon, South Korea:

The fourth-longest bridge in the world, the Incheon Bridge, links the mainland to Incheon International Airport.

A memorial that honors the Korean War landing action is called Incheon Landing Memorial Hall.

Chinatown is the biggest Chinatown in South Korea and is home to several authentic Chinese stores, eateries, and cultural activities.

Songdo Central Park is a sizable park with a lake, a musical fountain, and an artificial beach.

Contemporary Korean art is on display in the Incheon Skyart Museum, a museum in Incheon's Free Economic Zone.

The picturesque island of Muuido is well-known for its beaches and outdoor pursuits including hiking and fishing.

Popular Eulwangri Beach has a beautiful shoreline and plenty of opportunities for participating in water sports.

Wolmido Amusement Park is a vintage amusement park featuring a variety of thrilling rides and activities.

Places To Visit In JEJU

Popular tourist destination Jeju Island in South Korea is renowned for its stunning natural scenery and distinctive culture. Popular destinations include:

The tallest peak in South Korea is located in Hallasan National Park, a UNESCO World Heritage site, and there are many beautiful hiking paths there as well.

Seongsan Ilchulbong is a volcanic tuff cone with sweeping views of the ocean below.

Jeju Loveland is a sculpture park where a variety of pornographic works are on display.

Manjanggul Cave.: A lava tube cave with unusual rock formations

The Jeju Folklore & Natural History Museum: A museum that highlights the history and culture of Jeju Island is called.

Jeju Horse Ranch is a beautiful ranch that provides horseback riding classes and excursions.

The Jeju green tea industry's history and culture are on display at the O'sulloc Tea Museum.

Teddy Bear Museum:
Teddy bears and other plush animals are on display at the Jeju Cheonjiyeon

Waterfall is a beautiful waterfall situated in a verdant jungle.

Jeju World Cup Stadium is a sizable venue that hosts sporting events and football (soccer) games.

Locations To See In BUSAN

The coastal city of Busan in South Korea is well-known for its stunning beaches, mouthwatering cuisine, and extensive cultural history. Popular destinations include:

Haeundae Beach is a well-liked beach with beautiful ocean views and white sand.

Jagalchi Fish Market is a sizable fish market with plenty of eateries and snack stands.

Gamcheon Culture Village is a vibrant area with street art, murals, and charming eateries.

Beomeosa Temple is a revered Buddhist building in the highlands that has a long history.

Taejongdae Resort Park:
A picturesque park with lovely views of the sea, cliffs, and animals

Gwangalli Beach is a well-liked beach with a buzzing environment and plenty of food stands.

Busan Museum of Modern and Contemporary Art: Korean contemporary art is on display at the.

Haedong Yonggungsa Temple is a stunning Buddhist temple that is situated by the sea.

Busan International Film Festival (BIFF) Square is the primary location for the yearly Busan International Film Festival. It is located in the heart of Busan.

Nampo-dong is a crowded shopping area with many of boutiques, eateries, and food stands.

DESTINATIONS IN SOUTH KOREA THAT IS BEST FOR SOLO TRAVELERS

A lot of sights and activities are available for single travelers in South Korea, a well-liked vacation spot. Here are a few of South Korea's top destinations for lone travelers:

Jeju Island: Famous for its beautiful scenery, beaches, and natural marvels including Mount Hallasan, Manjanggul Cave, and Seongsan Ilchulbong, Jeju Island is a well-liked tourist destination.

Busan is a coastal city in the southeast of South Korea that is well-known for its stunning beaches, humming seafood markets, and exciting nightlife.

Gyeongju is a city in South Korea's southeast that is renowned for its extensive history and cultural heritage. The Bulguksa Temple, Anapji Pond, and Cheomseongdae Observatory are a some of Gyeongju's well-known sights.

Southwest South Korean city of Jeonju is renowned for its traditional architecture, thriving culinary scene, and charming streets. Jeonju's Hanok Village, Traditional Korean Wine Museum, and Traditional Food Street are a few of the city's most well-known attractions.

Andong: This city in South Korea's southeast is renowned for its illustrious past, enduring traditions, and picturesque surroundings. Andong Hahoe Folk Village, Dosan Confucian School, and Andong Mask Dance Drama Festival are a few of the city's well-known attractions.

These are just a handful of the many fantastic locations in South Korea that are ideal for solitary travelers. In this interesting nation, you're likely to discover something that suits your interests and style, whether you're drawn to its history and culture, beautiful landscapes, or lively cities.

CHAPTER 4 BANK CARDS AND CURRENCY

The Best Accepted South Korea Bank Cards

Most credit and debit cards from well-known global payment systems including Visa, Mastercard, and American Express are extensively accepted in South Korea.

However, it is advised to use a card from a local bank for a more smooth experience and to prevent any possible problems with card acceptance. The following are a few of the most well-known banks in South Korea and the brands of cards they issue:

KB Kookmin Bank - KB Kookmin Card Woori Bank - Woori Bank Card Shinhan Bank - Shinhan Card

Hana Card from Hana Bank

the Nonghyup Card from Nonghyup Bank

The majority of South Korean businesses, including shops, eateries, and internet retailers, accept these regional bank cards.
In conclusion, for a smoother experience with card acceptance, it is advised to use a local bank card from one of South Korea's well-known banks. However, significant global payment systems like Visa and Mastercard are also commonly used.

Best Locations In South Korea To Change Currencies To WON

There are several ways to convert foreign currencies into the South Korean Won, the country's official currency (KRW). The following are some of the top locations in South Korea to exchange currencies:

Banks: The majority of South Korea's big banks provide currency exchange services and have fair exchange rates. With locations all around the nation, banks including Shinhan Bank, KB Kookmin Bank, and Woori Bank are practical choices for currency conversion.

Currency Exchange Booths: Numerous currency exchange booths can be found in airports and other tourist destinations like Seoul's Myeong-dong and Insadong. Although these booths sometimes impose larger costs than banks do, they normally provide competitive exchange rates.

Online currency exchange services: A few online services, including TransferWise and currencyfair, allow you to convert currencies at competitive exchange rates and with little costs. They also transfer the South Korean Won to your bank account.

Hotels: South Korea has a large number of hotels that provide currency conversion services, however their exchange rates and costs could be less beneficial than those offered by banks and currency exchange booths.

In conclusion, there are several ways to convert foreign currencies into South Korean Won in that country, including banks, currency exchange booths, internet businesses, and hotels. To locate the best solution for your requirements, it's advised to check exchange rates and costs among several possibilities.

CHAPTER 5 K-ETA

Foreigners without a visa must apply for and get a K-ETA electronically before entering the Republic of Korea. To do so, they must provide the necessary information online, including their travel itinerary.

Travel should be made for work, pleasure, to see family, attend events, or meet with other people (excluding pursuit of profit).

All foreigners entering Korea from nations that do not need a visa or that grant them one must complete the K-ETA starting on September 1, 2021. (Within Ireland) Foreign nationals will not be allowed to board a flight to Korea if they do not have a K-ETA or a current visa. If your visa is still valid, you do not need a K-ETA.

Please be aware that the K-ETA website is located at k-eta.go.kr. Sites that are not official should be avoided.

A List Of Nations That Have K-ETA

Mexico, Monaco, New Caledonia, Nicaragua, Palau, Saint Kitts-Nevis, Saint Vincent and the Grenadines, Holy See, Albania, Andorra, Barbados, Dominica, Guam, Guyana, The following countries are included in this list: San Marino, Slovenia, the United Kingdom, the United States of America, Greece, the Netherlands, Denmark, Latvia, Romania, Luxembourg, Lithuania, Belgium, Bulgaria, Cyprus, Sweden, Spain, Slovakia, Estonia, Austria, Italy, the Czech Republic, Croatia, Portugal, Poland, France, Finland, Hungary, Norway, Switzerland, Liechtenstein, and Iceland.
Saudi Arabia, Kazakhstan, Qatar, Thailand, Turkey, Guatemala, Dominican Republic, Bahamas, Brazil, Saint Lucia, Suriname, Haiti, Antigua and Barbuda, United Arab Emirates, Bahrain, Oman Russia, Montenegro, Bosnia and Herzegovina, Serbia, Nauru, Marshall Islands,

Fiji, Tuvalu, Australia, Republic of South Africa, Lesotho, Morocco, Mauritius, Botswana, Seychelles, Eswatini, Canada, Argentina, Honduras, Paraguay,
Kuwait, Panama, Peru, New Zealand, Grenada, Brunei Darussalam, Saudi Arabia, and Honk Kong Solomon Islands, Kiribati, Tonga, Micronesia, Samoa, Taiwan, Macau, and Japan

Exceptions For Submitting An Application For The K-ETA

Only those with a UN passport, an ABTC, a USFK military member, an aircraft or ship crew member, a transfer passenger, or a traveler to Jeju Island using a direct flight are exempt from submitting an application for the K-ETA.

Holders of diplomatic or official passports won't need to submit a K-ETA application as of January 9, 2023.

K-ETA Application Procedure

- At the K-official ETA's website, www.k-eta.go.kr, you may submit an application (PC and mobile app)
- You must submit your K-ETA application at least 72 hours before boarding a ship or airplane to the Republic of Korea.
(As a result of the rise in K-ETA applications, the procedure is presently taking longer than 72 hours.)
* A proxy may fill out the application on your behalf. Up to 30 persons may be applied for simultaneously.

Requirements For The K-ETA

a current profile photo, an email address, and a valid passport are also required.

Check the result - You may check the result through email or online within 72 hours of submitting your application.

(Due to the increase in K-ETA applications, the process now takes longer than 72 hours.)

Validity Term

Starting on the date of approval, the validity lasts for two years.

Fees For The K-ETA

The price is 10,000 KRW ($9 to $10). (other fees not included).

Reapplication

Please be aware that after the application has been sent, the data entered cannot be altered. Even if your current K-ETA is still valid, you must reapply if you entered incorrect information or changed the information you entered regarding your name, sex, date of birth, nationality, passport information (passport number or expiration date), criminal history, and infectious disease information.

Those in possession of a current K-ETA are exempt from having to fill out the arrival card.

For your knowledge and clarification, K-ETA IS NOT A VISA. K-ETA approval does not guarantee Republic of Korea admission; the final decision will be made by a Korea Immigration Service representative at the port of entry. Please contact the appropriate agency for further information on the requirements since the K-ETA center is not in charge of quarantine. (1339)

Complete Travel Advice:

local laws

You may apply online for a K-ETA (or visa waiver) for travel to South Korea. The K-ETA application must be submitted at least 72 hours before departure. Conditions for admission and exit might abruptly alter. Contact the South Korean embassy or consulate that is most convenient for you for the most latest information.

You are not need to take a pre-departure COVID-19 test or a PCR test upon arrival to enter South Korea unless you are traveling from China, Hong Kong, or Macau.

Passengers departing from China, Hong Kong, or Macau must provide a negative COVID-19 test result before boarding their flight to South Korea. This might either be a PCR test done up to 48 hours before your departure or a supervised RAT test done up to 24 hours before your flight.

Every visitor entering South Korea from China, Hong Kong, or Macau must do a PCR test immediately and isolate themselves while they wait for the results. Foreign nationals must take the test immediately. Korean nationals and long-term residents are both qualified to take the exam straight immediately.

If your COVID-19 status is confirmed upon arrival, you must self-isolate at home if you are a Korean citizen or long-term resident, or you must isolate for 7 days in a government facility.

You should register your personal information with the Korean Q-code registration system at the Q-code website before coming to South Korea. Then, you'll get a created QR code upon your arrival. Passengers coming from China, Hong Kong, or Macau must register using the Q-code system before to boarding.

CHAPTER 6: THINGS YOU SHOULD KNOW

Informations Visitors Need To Know

A visa may be required for certain visitors from certain nations in order to enter South Korea. It's essential to learn about the requirements beforehand and to apply for a visa long before the trip.

The country's currency is the South Korean won (KRW). Banks, airports, and hotels all provide currency exchange services, as well as ATMs and credit cards.

Transportation: South Korea has well-developed rail, air, road, and local transportation networks. Visitors may choose the option that best satisfies their needs in terms of pricing and convenience.

Visitors should take steps to maintain their health, including drinking only bottled water, using bug repellent, and receiving vaccinations. Precautions for personal protection should also be taken, such as avoiding crime-ridden areas and locking up valuables.

Conversation: While English is widely spoken in South Korea, it may be good for travelers to learn some fundamental Korean words and phrases to facilitate communication. Visitors also have the option of purchasing a local SIM card or connecting to public Wi-Fi to remain connected.

Entry Procedures For Foreign Visitors

Certain entrance requirements must be met before entering South Korea, including:

1 Visa requirements: Depending on your place of origin and the reason for your travel, different

visas are needed to enter South Korea. On the website for Korean immigration, you may find out what kind of visas are needed in your country.

2 Health and quarantine requirements: All visitors to South Korea must go through health inspections and may need to stay in quarantine for a certain amount of time, depending on the situation.

3 Travel restrictions: There may be limitations on travel to and from certain nations depending on the COVID-19 status in both your home country and South Korea. On the website of the Korean government, you may find the most recent travel restrictions.

4 Proof of further travel: In order to enter South Korea, visitors may be asked to provide proof of onward travel, such as a return ticket or a ticket to another location.

5 Travel insurance: It is advised that visitors to South Korea get travel insurance, which may cover unanticipated medical costs as well as other travel-related problems.

6 Passport and other travel documents: In order to enter South Korea, you will need a passport that is currently valid as well as any other visas that may be required. Before departing, be sure to check the expiry dates on your passport and other travel papers to make sure they are still valid.

Before your travel, it's crucial to confirm the most recent South Korean entrance criteria since they are subject to change.

Rules To Follow as a Tourist or Foreigner

To guarantee a safe and pleasurable journey, it's crucial for tourists and foreign visitors to South Korea to be knowledgeable of the local traditions, laws, and regulations. The following are some laws that visitors and foreign nationals should be aware of:

1 Respect local traditions: South Korea has a rich cultural past, and tourists should observe this by abstaining from public displays of love and taking off their shoes before entering someone's house.

2 Follow traffic regulations: South Korea has rigorous traffic regulations, so travelers must abide by them whether driving or walking on the roadways.

3 Do not leave rubbish lying around: It is against the law to leave trash lying around in South Korea, and tourists are required to dispose of their trash correctly in designated trash cans.

4 Respect for personal space: South Korea places a high emphasis on privacy, so visitors should show respect for others' privacy by refraining from being too noisy or invasive in public areas.

5 Do not participate in criminal activity. South Korea rigorously prohibits unlawful activity, and violators may face harsh repercussions. Illegal activity includes drug use, theft, and vandalism.

6 Make responsible use of public transportation: Travelers should make responsible use of public transportation, such as buses and trains, by refraining from disruptive conduct and respecting the rights of other passengers.

7 Respect wildlife. South Korea is home to a variety of animals. Tourists should respect the wildlife by avoiding damaging their habitats or taking part in activities that might endanger them.

8 Restrictions on smoking: Smoking is not permitted in a lot of public areas, including pubs, restaurants, and public transportation. Before lighting up, visitors should make sure they are in a recognized smoking location.

9 Dress code: Visitors are advised to respect local traditions and customs by dressing properly while attending formal events or visiting religious sites.

10 When taking pictures of people or locations, particularly at cultural or religious institutions, visitors should always obtain permission.

11 Tipping: Since it's not customary in South Korea to leave tips in restaurants or cabs, tourists shouldn't feel pressured to do so.

12 Use of credit cards: Credit cards are generally accepted in South Korea, although travelers should be aware of the currency rates and costs when using credit cards and should check with their bank for information on overseas transactions.

13 Visitors visiting South Korea should be aware of the country's emergency services, especially the emergency number (119), which may be

used to contact the police, fire department, or ambulance services.

14 Take things with both hands.

In South Korea, being courteous is something that everyone does all the time. If you're a tourist and you come across a restaurant, convenience shop, etc., don't forget to use both hands to collect the change that has been provided to you by the merchant or the cashier. This displays politeness. It is usually nice to use your two hands, say thank you, and bow when receiving anything from someone; therefore, you may do this in situations other than those described above.

15 Before entering someone's home, remove your shoes.

Most Asian nations engage in this activity on a regular basis. In certain circumstances, you must take off your shoes before entering a person's home or restaurant in Korea. Keep in mind that this is important because if you neglect to take off your shoes, you can encounter disappointed looks from Koreans since it is seen as impolite.

16 Segregate your garbage.

Don't discard your trash somewhere when visiting Korea. When it comes to this, Koreans are very precise. Third in the world in terms of recycling rates is South Korea. It's crucial that you separate your garbage into ordinary trash and recyclables. If you are caught improperly tossing your garbage, be prepared to witness unhappy faces.

17 Discover the fundamental terms of Korean.

It is advised to learn a few basic Korean terms before traveling to South Korea. No worries; learning a few lines, phrases, and words will be enough; you don't need to master the whole language and its syntax. Even if you can't speak in complete sentences but know some basic vocabulary (related to travel), Koreans will usually understand you.When visiting South Korea, you may find the following basic Korean terms useful:

Where? — Eodie/Eodi-ye

What amount? — Eolmayeyo

I'm grateful. Kamsahamnida

Jwesonghamnida: "I'm sorry."

Hello, Annyeonghaseyo.

18 When dialing a cab, use your palm.

Perhaps surprisingly, Koreans don't use a single finger to dial a cab. To them, it is seen as impolite. Even though it's just a tiny favor, the Korean people will value it if you do this.

CHAPTER 7:
TRANSPORTATION

Transportation in South korea

A. Air travel: Incheon International Airport and Gimpo International Airport, South Korea's two largest international airports, act as hubs for both domestic and foreign flights. Travelers may swiftly and comfortably get to several tourist attractions in South Korea by flying to major cities inside the country.

B. Rail Transportation: South Korea's rail network is broad and functional, providing tourists with a practical and economical means of transportation. The nation's high-speed rail system, known as the KTX, links the main cities and offers a fast and convenient means of long-distance travel. Regional trains and subways are also available, and they provide quick access to tourist destinations in metropolitan regions.

Road Travel: Travelers who like to drive in South Korea may hire a vehicle and take advantage of the flexibility to see the nation at their own leisure. Although the nation boasts a vast network of highways and roads, traffic in metropolitan areas may be heavy, so travelers should be prepared for slower speeds.

D. Local Transportation: South Korea's local transportation network, which consists of buses, subways, and taxis, is well developed. Buses are widely accessible and provide a practical and affordable way to explore both urban and rural locations. Particularly in metropolitan locations, subways are quick and practical, while cabs are commonly accessible and provide a flexible mode of transportation.

E. Driving in South Korea: Travelers who want to drive in South Korea should be aware of local driving rules and practices. The right side of the road is used for driving, and everyone in the vehicle must wear a seatbelt. Additionally, visitors should get acquainted with traffic signs and be ready for severe traffic in metropolitan locations. If you want to drive in South Korea, you need an international driving permit.

The Easiest Form Of Transportation In Sour Korea

The most convenient mode of transportation in South Korea depends on the traveler's preferences, financial constraints, and final location. However, it's generally agreed that the following choices are the most practical ones:

Subway: The vast, quick, and reasonably priced subway system in South Korea It is regarded as one of the greatest in the world and includes coverage of significant cities, including Seoul, Busan, and Incheon.

Taxi: For shorter journeys, taxis are a practical and generally accessible choice in South Korea. They may be hailed on the street or at a taxi stand, and they are very fairly priced.

THE KAKOA TAXI

In South Korea, Kakao Taxi is a taxi-hailing service that utilizes the Kakao app. The app links customers with authorized taxi drivers and offers real-time data on the whereabouts and condition of accessible cabs.

Kakao Taxi's features include the following:

Booking a cab is simple thanks to the Kakao app, which allows users to enter their pick-up and drop-off points.

Real-time information: The app allows users to follow the progress of their journey by providing real-time information on the location and status of available taxis.

Kakao Taxi offers a variety of payment options, including cash and credit/debit cards.

Information on the driver is provided via the app to promote passenger safety and trust. This information includes the driver's name, picture, and rating.

Customer service: Kakao Taxi provides round-the-clock customer service to resolve any queries or issues.

The Usual Method of Paying Kokao Taxi

In South Korea, credit or debit cards that have been processed using the Kakao app are the standard form of payment for Kakao Taxi. Following the completion of the trip, the fare is immediately charged to the saved card, and an email receipt is also issued to the user.

Cash, Kakao Pay, and mobile banking applications are just a few of the other payment options that Kakao Taxi provides. Before scheduling a ride, users may choose their preferred payment option via the app.

South Korea uses Kakao Taxi often and is renowned for its dependable, quick, and convenient service. It is a well-liked substitute for conventional taxi services and a practical choice for individuals who like using a smartphone app to both reserve and pay for their journeys.

The Difference Between the Blue and General Taxis

There are primarily two sorts of taxis in South Korea: blue taxis and regular taxis. The main distinctions between them are as follows:

Price structure: Compared to regular taxis, blue taxis often have a higher base cost and a smaller per-kilometer fee. They may be more cost-effective for longer excursions, but are often more costly for shorter ones.

Regions of service: Blue taxis are only permitted in big cities; they are not permitted to pick up customers in rural areas. Contrarily, general taxis may pick up people in both urban and rural settings.

Blue taxis often feature more modern, higher-end automobile types, and they frequently offer conveniences like GPS and credit card readers. General taxis may have fewer amenities and older vehicle types.

Driver education: In comparison to regular taxi drivers, blue cab drivers must undergo extra training and adhere to stricter requirements.

Customer service: Blue taxis are renowned for providing excellent customer service and are often thought of as more dependable and trustworthy than regular taxis.

Booking options: While regular taxis may also be booked over the phone or via ride-hailing applications like Kakao Taxi, blue taxis can only be hailed from the street.

Blue taxis are often delivered more swiftly than regular taxis, which results in a shorter waiting period.

Blue taxis are a preferable choice for those who have a lot of luggage since they often have greater luggage space than regular taxis.

GPS and navigation systems are available in blue taxis, which might be helpful for customers who are unfamiliar with the neighborhood. These characteristics may not be present in regular taxis.

Comfort: Compared to regular taxis, blue taxis often provide a greater degree of comfort, including more roomy and comfortable seats, superior air conditioning, and other amenities.

In conclusion, a person's requirements and preferences will determine whether they choose a blue taxi or a regular cab. While regular taxis are more accessible and may be more cost-effective for shorter journeys, blue taxis provide higher-quality service and cars but are often more costly.

Bus: Another practical mode of transportation inside South Korea, particularly over longer distances, is the bus. They serve both urban and rural regions and provide a less expensive alternative to trains and taxis.

South Korea's KTX Train

The Korean State Railway runs the high-speed KTX (Korea Train Express) railway system in

South Korea. It was originally established in 2004 and links Busan, Daejeon, Gwangju, and other significant South Korean cities with Seoul, the country's capital.

Here are some of the KTX train's main characteristics:

Speed: The KTX trains are among the fastest in the world, with top speeds of 300 km/h.

Routes: The Gyeongbu Line, Honam Line, and Jeolla Line are just a few of the major lines that the KTX uses.

Trains leave from Seoul Station multiple times an hour for different locations, and they operate regularly.

Convenience: The KTX trains are furnished with contemporary conveniences, including air conditioning, cozy seats, and food and beverage services.

Convenience: Given that they let passengers avoid traffic and get to their destinations more quickly, KTX trains provide a handy method to get between cities.

In general, the KTX is well-liked by both residents and visitors in South Korea and is regarded as a reliable and effective method of transportation.

Requirements for Obtaining a KTX Train Ticket

The following basic conditions must be met in order to purchase a ticket for the South Korean KTX train:

Identification: In order to buy a ticket, you must have a legitimate, government-issued picture ID, such as a passport or national ID card.

Payment options include cash, credit or debit cards, and KTX tickets.

Standard-class and first-class KTX tickets are two of the several ticket classes that are offered. You may choose the ticket type that best suits your requirements and financial situation.

Reservation of a seat: You may reserve a seat in person or online. You may still buy a ticket and take any open seat if you don't have a reservation.

Stations of departure and arrival: When buying your ticket, be sure to indicate the stations of departure and arrival.

Date and time of travel: You must also provide the date and time of your trip.

It is advised to reserve your KTX ticket in advance to guarantee availability, particularly during periods of high travel demand. Remember that the cost of the tickets may change based on the day and season.

The Difference Between a KTX First-Class Ticket and a Standard-Class Ticket

The following are the primary distinctions between first-class and normal-class KTX tickets in South Korea:

Comfort: First-class seating is more roomy and pleasant than ordinary-class seating, with larger seats, greater legroom, and better reclining choices.

Price: First-class tickets often cost more than tickets for other classes. Depending on the route and hour of travel, there may be a precise pricing variation.

First-class passengers often get extra perks, including complimentary food and beverages, as well as access to VIP lounges at certain stations.

Privacy: Compared to normal class, first class cabins often feature fewer seats per row and provide greater privacy.

First-class tickets might be hard to come by and could sell out more quickly, particularly during busy travel periods.

In conclusion, first class may be a suitable alternative if comfort and privacy are essential to you and you're willing to pay a premium. Standard class on the KTX is still a pleasant and practical choice if you're on a tight budget, however.

PROCESS OF BOOKING A FERRY

There are various methods to purchase a ferry ticket in South Korea, where ferries are a well-liked means of transportation. Here are a few such approaches:

Online purchasing: You may purchase a ticket in advance on the websites of several ferry companies. Visit the website of the ferry company, choose the route, the dates, and the time you want, then finish the payment procedure.

Travel agencies: If you're planning a longer journey, booking a ferry ticket via a travel agency is a simple option. Just choose a travel firm that specializes in South Korean tourism and request that they arrange for the reservation of your boat ticket.

Directly at the ferry port: If you would rather buy your ticket in person, you may stop by the ferry terminal and do it at the ticket counter.

By phone: You may purchase your ticket over the phone using certain ferry operators' telephone booking services. To reserve your ticket, just dial the you ferry operator's customer service line and follow the instructions.

Check the departure and arrival times, the availability of various service classes, and the terms of the tariff, including any extra taxes or surcharges, before purchasing your ferry ticket.

Tips for Traveling With Infants to South Korea

Selecting Flights

When it was feasible, choosing an overnight journey helped me the most with setting up a peaceful and manageable travel as well as with assisting my young child in adjusting to a new timeslot. Avoiding sweets and naps the day before the journey, as well as clothing your children in cozy pajamas for bed, might help set the mood for the night if you are able to book an overnight flight.

Being Comfortable

It is better for everyone if you make your child feel at ease throughout a protracted travel. Although the FAA advises safety restraints for kids under 40 pounds, you shouldn't take it for granted that your car seat has FAA approval. My one-year-old typically slept well in the car seat, so I were dismayed to see that mine wasn't. Always double-check.

I bought a CARES, or Child Aviation Restraint System, that has FAA approval. Although the straps seem to be difficult, they are really rather easy to use, and flight attendants are always there to assist you. Additionally, CARES works on excursions that you could want to take while in Korea as well as bus journeys, including the shuttle bus to Camp Humphreys.

I carried an inflatable travel footrest with me on the journey, and it fit well in front of the seat on Korean Carriers aircraft, which had far more leg space than some other airlines, including Delta. On my Delta flights, the inflated footrest just fit. The footrest extends the seat when it is completely inflated, like a tiny bed. I was really appreciative that this suggestion came directly from Facebook mothers. The majority of the nine-hour journey was spent in sleep for our infant, who sometimes curled up in a ball and used the footrest as a pillow and occasionally as a footrest. This choice may not be the most convenient if your kid is tall.

Once again, Korean Airlines comes through with the pillows and blankets, and this time it worked for my journey home. Another alternative was to lay a tiny cushion on each arm rest. They immediately fell asleep once I sat back in the chair.

Entertainment during flying

Traveling with infants and young children is made much simpler by having comfortable headphones that may be used for amusement as well as noise cancellation. When compared to the availability of music, audiobooks, and screen entertainment throughout the trip, none of the window clings, travel magnets, activity books, magnetic erase boards, dry erase books, or color wonder mess-free pens I had bought could compete. Bring before the trip some of your child's favorite activities. Keep in mind that you also need to get as much sleep and relax as you can.

think about making low-cost craft items that are simple to pack before departing, such making your own dry-erase boards out of cardboard and clear packing tape. Perhaps a nice activity to perform a month or two beforehand with your kid.

Food choices

As long as they don't include more than 3.4 ounces of liquid or cream, bring snacks that your infants or young children will love while traveling. The Western and Korean food selections on Korean Airlines were helpful for my picky kid and myself.I had to prepare toddler-approved meals and snacks for our non-Korean Airlines flights. Stock up on pricey airport alternatives right now.

You should be able to pack a cooler with ice to keep bottles if you're traveling with young children. Of course, you'll need to carry the formula and buy water after the TSA check is over. Travelers with young children may use the TSA's special screening section at Incheon Airport, which has a considerably shorter wait.

creating a backup strategy for the aircraft

Adults don't often consider how children, who may also have difficulty expressing their demands verbally, feel changes in cabin pressure. As the aircraft was coming in for a landing, my child began crying because her ears ached. They were alright when I offered them a lollipop since they aren't used to eating gum.

As always, be prepared for spills by having additional clothing, wipes, and slip-on diapers on hand. On the flight to Korea, I made an effort to keep our one-year-old hydrated, but it led to diaper overflow.

ACCOMMODATION ARRANGEMENTS IN SOUTH KOREA

Types of Accommodation: South Korea provides a variety of lodging alternatives, from contemporary hotels and resorts to historic inns built in the Korean style (hanok). Guesthouses and hostels are affordable choices for travelers, while five-star hotels and resorts provide luxurious accommodations.

B. Popular Places to Stay: There are many different places to stay in South Korea's main cities, including Seoul, Busan, and Incheon, with alternatives to fit every budget and taste. Visitors have the option of staying in the busy city areas, where they are close to eating, shopping, and entertainment, or choosing calmer districts that are conveniently located near public transit.

Affordable Alternatives: For travelers wishing to save costs on lodging, South Korea offers a variety of affordable options. Budget hotels, guesthouses, and hostels provide straightforward, spotless lodging at reasonable rates. Traditional Korean-style rooms are available in certain guesthouses, although Western-style rooms with communal bathrooms are also available.

D. Luxurious Accommodations: South Korea offers a wide selection of five-star hotels and resorts for tourists searching for luxurious lodging. These include opulent lodgings and amenities, including spas, dining options, and workout facilities. Traditional Korean-style inns are another option for tourists since they provide a distinctive and genuine experience. Major cities like Seoul and well-liked tourist sites like Jeju Island are home to some of the world's greatest luxury lodgings.

Good Hotels In Myeongdong

1, IBIS STYLE AMBASSADOR
2, NINE TREE
3, RAMADA NAMEDAEMUN
4, HENNA-NA HOTEL
5, WESTERN CHOSUN

Good Hotels In JEJU

1, PARNAS HOTEL
2, JEJU SHINHWA WORLD LAND   RESORT
3 PHOENIX SEOPJIKOJI
4, THE SHILLA
5, LOTTE HOTEL

Good Hotels In Busan

1, SIGNIEL BUSAN
2, AVANI CENTRAL
3, PARADISE
4, ASTI HOTEL BUSAN STATION

Good Hotels In Incheon

1, OAKWOOD PREMIER IN INCHEON
2, GRAND HIGH INCHEON
3, GOLDEN TULIP INCHEON AIRPORT HOTEL

4, SHERATON GRAND AND INCHEON HOTELS
5, DAYS HOTEL AND SUIT INCHEON AIRPORT

Good Hotels In Hongdae

1, ALOFT SEOUL GANGNAM
2, L7 HONGDAE
3, HOLIDAY IN
4, LOTTE CITY MAPO
5, BRICK

CHAPTER 8: SOUTH KOREA'S FOOD AND DRINK

A. Korean cuisine is renowned for its strong tastes, natural ingredients, and wide variety of meals. Korean cuisine, which includes everything from grilled meat to fermented veggies, is delectable and nutritious, making it a must-try for tourists.

B. Popular Cuisines: Some of the most well-known Korean dishes include bibimbap (rice bowl with meat and veggies), kimchi, and bulgogi (marinated beef) (spicy fermented vegetables). Samgyeopsal (grilled pig belly), japchae (stir-fried noodles with veggies), and tteokbokki are some recommended dishes for tourists to sample (spicy rice cakes).

C. Local Beverages: South Korean beverages include tea, soju, and traditional rice wine known as makgeolli (green tea is particularly popular). Sikhye, a sweet and energizing rice beverage, and herbal teas like ginger tea and citron tea are other recommended drinks for tourists to sample.

D. Dining Etiquette: It's crucial to observe local customs while dining in South Korea. For instance, using chopsticks to eat is usual, yet sticking them upright in a bowl of rice is frowned upon. Additionally, visitors should refrain from speaking while chewing food and should utilize the designated serving utensils rather than reaching across the table for food. Furthermore, it is crucial to hold off on beginning to eat until the oldest person at the table does so.

FANTASTIC RESTAURANTS IN SEOUL

With a vast variety of eating alternatives for all tastes and price ranges, Seoul, South Korea is renowned for its rich culinary culture and eclectic food scene. Here are a few Seoul eateries that come highly recommended:

The rotating restaurant at Namsan Seoul Tower offers a unique eating experience and breathtaking views over the city. While dining there, you may take in sweeping panoramas of the area.

Visit Gwangjang Market, a lively food market with a variety of street food shops selling everything from bibimbap to kimchi stew, for a taste of traditional Korean cuisine.

Visit Sanchon, a restaurant that specializes in meals crafted with fresh, seasonal ingredients, for a taste of traditional Korean temple cuisine.

Goryeo-era Royal Food is a highly recommended restaurant that serves a variety of meals made in the Goryeo Dynasty's manner if you're interested in sampling classic royal Korean cuisine.

Hanjan: If you're looking for modern Korean cuisine, this highly regarded eatery puts a modern twist on classic Korean dishes made using locally sourced seasonal ingredients.

Toc Toc: Toc Toc is a well-recommended Korean fried chicken business that provides a range of tastes and dipping sauces for a relaxed and inexpensive eating experience.

These are just a handful of Seoul's many fantastic restaurants. Regardless of the food you choose, this bustling and varied city is guaranteed to have something to suit your taste.

CHAPTER 9

SOUTH KOREA'S HEALTH AND SAFETY

Safety Precautions:

Although South Korea is typically a safe place for travelers, tourists should nevertheless exercise care. Pickpocketing and theft need must be avoided by visitors, particularly in busy places like marketplaces, subways, and tourist attractions. Visitors should use care while using ATMs since card skimming and cloning are frequent. Another smart move is to store priceless items and critical papers in a hotel safe or other safe place.

Health Considerations:

Travelers visiting South Korea should be aware of the possible health concerns, such as food poisoning, air pollution, and illnesses spread by insects. In particular during the sweltering and humid summer months, visitors should take care to prevent heat exhaustion and sunstroke. Bring enough sunscreen, bug repellent, and a hat, it is advised. Additionally, visitors should be careful to only consume bottled water, avoid adding ice to their beverages, and maintain proper cleanliness.

Emergency Contact Numbers:

Foreigners visiting South Korea should dial 112 for the police, 119 for the ambulance, and 1339 for tourist information in the case of an emergency. Along with knowing where the closest hospital or medical institution is, visitors should always carry a list of emergency phone numbers with them. Visitors can also inquire about emergency medical coverage and evacuation from their travel insurance provider.

SCAM ALERTS

Unofficial Websites For The K-ETA
Application

Unofficial K-ETA application websites were
recently found to be charging more than was
necessary. One website charged for the K-ETA
application even 20 times more than the stated
price.

Application is only accepted via the official
K-ETA website (www.k-eta.go.kr) and mobile
app (K-ETA). The Republic of Korea's
government has not approved any application
agency for K-ETA.

The 10,000KRW (extra charge omitted) K-ETA
fee is the only cost involved. Additionally, from
May 3 through August 31 (the trial project
period), the K-ETA application fee is waived.

Please proceed with the utmost care to avoid any financial losses or frauds that may be caused by illegitimate application agencies.

When planning a trip to South Korea, there are a few common scams to be aware of.
To prevent any unpleasant shocks when traveling to South Korea, it's crucial to be aware of possible scams. Here are a few typical frauds to be on the lookout for:

Taxi drivers overcharging tourists: Some cabbies may attempt to take advantage of visitors by overcharging for trips or taking longer routes to raise the fee. Use a trustworthy ride-hailing service, or be sure to request that the meter be switched on to prevent this.

Fake goods: Street sellers may advertise and sell knockoff designer clothing and accessories as authentic things. Prevent purchasing anything from street sellers in order to avoid being conned. Only purchase items from recognized retailers.

ATM skimming: Thieves may install skimming equipment on ATMs to steal bank account funds and card data. Use ATMs that are only found in banks or in busy, well-lit places to prevent this, and always cover the keypad while entering your PIN.

Fraudulent currency exchange services: It's crucial to examine rates at different services and only use reputed services since certain firms may give disadvantageous exchange rates or charge hidden costs.

Scams involving timeshares: Some scammers could pretend to be salesmen and approach visitors with offers to buy timeshares or real estate investment opportunities. Use only licensed, recognized real estate brokers and be skeptical of unsolicited offers to prevent this.

Free tours or presents: Some people could approach travelers and offer free tours or gifts, but they'll later demand money or try to sell them expensive goods. Use only authorized and recognized tour guides to prevent this, and be wary of unsolicited pitches.

Phone or Wi-Fi scams: Unsecure public Wi-Fi networks might be used by thieves to steal personal information or infect devices with malware. Use only reputable Wi-Fi networks and stay away from critical online transactions like online banking and shopping on public Wi-Fi to prevent this.

Pickpocketing: It's crucial to store valuables and critical papers, including passports and credit cards, in a safe location since theft and pickpocketing may be issues in tourist locations.

Unlicensed taxis: It's crucial to always utilize licensed taxi services since unlicensed taxis may not be safe and may not be insured.

You may assist guarantee a risk-free and pleasurable vacation to South Korea by being watchful and informed of these possible frauds.

It's crucial to inform the local authorities if you think you may have fallen victim to a scam.

CHAPTER 10 BEST KOREA SIM CARD FOR TRAVELERS IN 2023

The complete list of Korea travel SIM cards that can be booked in advance and picked up at the airport

It is also possible to have the SIM delivered to your house or pick it up at the departure airport in various Asian nations, like Singapore, Malaysia, and Indonesia to mention a few.
I can honestly declare that using a Korea data SIM card from KT Olleh was a great benefit since I used one myself

I put a ton of different Korean applications onto my phone in addition to using superb navigational apps like Naver apps (Google Maps is mostly worthless in South Korea). I was able to decipher Korean messages, eat where the locals ate, and communicate with Koreans considerably more easily as a result of these applications.

List of Applications you'll Need When Traveling in South Korea

The following applications were my favorites when I was driving in South Korea:

The South Korean Won and your native currency may be converted in real time with XE CURRENC.

You are guided through Seoul's spaghetti-like subway system by KAKAO METRO.
Additionally, the app functions in Daegu, Busan, Gwangju, and Daejeon.
Similar to Uber, KAKAO T allows you to call and pay for a taxi. You may even hire an electric bike with it.

MANGOPLATE, details on the neighborhood eateries, including reviews

With Papago, you can translate South Korean quickly and accurately into 13 other languages, including English, French, German, Japanese, and Chinese. It is offline-compatible and produces translations of higher quality than Google Translate.

The Interior and Safety Ministry app called Emergency Ready. The app includes details about police, fire, and shelter stations. In the event of a typhoon or other natural catastrophe, the government will provide updates. (App Store - Google Play)

The Korea Tourism Organization provides the app Visit Korea. Opening times, costs, and a wealth of other helpful details on the several rural attractions are all included.

You may use the apps from Lotte World or Everland to monitor the wait times at the attractions if you visit such theme parks.

ROAMING

Insane roaming fees and reasonably priced prepaid SIM cards are available in Korea. Even if you won't use your data connection every day, this makes it a wise investment.

It would be a pity not to use South Korea's superior 4G network while you are there. Larger cities like Seoul have a large number of WiFi hotspots as well.

Seoul Skypark attractions with free WiFi Some Seoul attractions provide free WiFi.

Wi-Fi is free in Korea

In Seoul alone, there are more than 500,000 public WiFi stations. You would assume that a data connection is an unnecessary luxury given this quantity, but it turns out that this was not the case.

First of all, it is a nuisance to repeatedly register your phone at new hotspots that you find. It wouldn't be such a huge deal if it ended there. However, certain registration forms are only available in Korean, making the process more difficult. Then, to make matters worse, you could discover that they only take Korean phone numbers once you have finally figured out the form.

Do not assume that there are no working WiFi hotspots for travellers.
You may utilize free WiFi hotspots, most notably in hotels and restaurants, but you shouldn't be taken aback by these staggering statistics.

The best options for SIM cards from South Korea

Korea travel SIMs are available from KT Olleh and SK Telecom.

In addition, a number of other service providers provide their own travel SIM cards that may be purchased overseas and that function in South Korea as well.

For all stays of 30 days or less when a data connection is all you require, this KT Olleh card provided by Klook is the perfect option.

A fair use guideline is not specified and the SIM offers limitless data. Even if there is one, it is fair to presume that the first 3GB of data per day will be at 4G/LTE rates even if there may not be one. More than adequate space for everyday usage is 3 GB.

You may extend your rental online if your plans change and you need to.

The Best Tourist SIM For Longer Stays

For extended stays

The average SIM card's lifetime is 30 days. If you want to remain in Korea for a period of time longer than 30 days, you will either need to purchase additional SIM cards—something that not all service providers permit—or extend your lease. Choosing this SIM card from KT Olleh, which is good for up to 90 days, is the simplest choice.

Both data-lite and data-heavy users have alternatives. The other option gives 10GB of 4G/LTE data, while the data-lite plan offers 300MB of fast data per month. Both plans provide limitless 3 Mbps data once the threshold is achieved.
Text messages and voice calls are also available, but you must top-up your SIM first.

for telephone calls

All of the SIM cards we discuss in this post support Skype or other comparable calling services, but there are certain situations when a regular phone call is still preferable.

You must purchase a voice+text-compatible KT Olleh SIM card to do this.

It should be noted that some of them only permit domestic calls. Other SIMS that provide voice calls often only offer local calling, whereas SIM cards that you fill up typically allow international calls.

These are the international call rates from KT.

Klook and Trazy both accept pre-orders for these SIM cards.

When placing a preorder via Klook, you must top up your own SIM card.

The pre-ordered SIMs from Trazy will come with a KRW 11,000 initial balance, which is adequate for around 42 minutes of domestic calling. If extra credits are required, you may add them.

Both choices cost about the same. At the time of writing, 11,000 KRW is equivalent to 7 USD, and the preloaded SIM is likewise 7 USD more costly than the other one. In other words, selecting the preconfigured choice is only a convenience and does not provide any financial benefits. You don't need to bother about the top-up procedure and may start contacting straight away.

You must choose the "data + domestic call and texts (additional topup)" bundle option on Klook.

The SIMs provide limitless data along with phone calls. 3GB of high-speed internet per day plus limitless bandwidth at 5Mbps are the limits set by Trazy. There is no indication of a fair use policy on Klook. This is more than enough for the majority of users, assuming it is the same.

Verify costs and availability:

KT Olleh text and voice SIM Klook SIM Trazy KT Olleh voice and text

South Korea's KT Olleh SIM

Which is better: a KT Olleh Tourist SIM for South Korea, or a data SIM?

Both are excellent methods for maintaining contact.
It can be simpler to utilize a WiFi device since all you have to do is switch it on and connect to the WiFi signal being broadcast. Of course, it adds another thing to carry about.

Pros and disadvantages for each are listed below.

Mobile WiFi in Korea

The biggest benefit of using a portable WiFi device is that you won't have to exchange SIM cards or alter any phone settings. To prevent any unpleasant data roaming penalties, you only need to make sure that your data connection is turned off.
The fact that friends, family, coworkers, and anybody else who has your phone number will be able to call you as if you were at home is

another benefit of this, which is wonderful if you're not very tech-savvy.

This is most likely the best choice if you wish to be reachable at all times.
The ability to share the internet connection is an additional benefit. Some gadgets only allow three simultaneous connections, while others allow up to ten. Some smartphones include a hotspot feature that does the same thing, however in our experience, this feature rapidly depletes the battery of the phone.
The main drawback of a portable WiFi gadget is that it adds another piece of equipment to your bag and requires daily charging if you use it regularly.

People won't be able to call you on your home carrier's number after you insert the local tourist SIM into your phone. It's time for a trip after all, so this could be a godsend.

A SIM card is still, by far, the most practical choice if you're traveling alone or won't be sharing the connection with anybody else and don't mind severing the cord with the home front for the length of your vacation.

Everyone will still be able to reach you using Skype and other comparable services like Google Hangouts. If you'd like, you may also use a SIM that enables voice+data.

If you choose such a SIM, you will get a local phone number that you may provide to family members back home.

An overview of the various South Korean tourist SIM card

To assist you in selecting the option that best meets your requirements, all the pertinent information is provided.

The world's fastest 4G network is in South Korea. No matter which network you choose, you will be able to browse at rates that are probably unattainable at home.

LG U+, SK Telecom, and KT are South Korea's three mobile service providers. They all provide the nation with outstanding coverage. With a coverage rate of 99.5%, LG U+ triumphs, while two other providers also reach at least 95%.

A stunning 40 Mbps is the average download speed, and SK Telecom even surpasses that with 65 Mbps. Additionally, upload speeds are really quick.

With the networks of SK Telecom and LG U+, you'll get at least 10 Mbps, with peaks of up to 15 Mbps.
These statistics are just provided to demonstrate that when selecting your SIM card, you shouldn't be too concerned with the operator.

What to look for and Consider When Purchasing a Korean Travel SIM

You can trust that a Korean Pocket WiFi gadget you hire will function. To prevent unpleasant surprises, you should do a few checks before purchasing a vacation SIM.

Here is a list of the details you should go through before making your purchase.

What to know before purchasing a South Korean SIM card
Be careful to examine these 3 aspects of your phone.

If you Google "technical specifications X," replacing X with the model of your phone, you should be able to get all the information you want.

What size SIM card do you require?
The size of SIM cards has shrunk over time. Modern smartphones utilize the Micro-SIM and the Nano-SIM, but older devices used the conventional SIM.

The majority of Korean travel SIM cards are so-called multi-size SIMs, which can be adjusted to the necessary size.

With these multi-size SIMs, you can't go wrong, but if the operator only sells Nano SIMs (as some do), you should make sure this is the proper size for your phone in advance.
You may check the technical requirements or open your phone to see what sort of SIM you need.

Your phone must be unlocked.
Locked phones will not function in South Korea since they are pre-installed with software that forbids using them on another network.

By phoning your phone provider, you may be able to unlock your locked phone.

In Europe, phone locking is uncommon, however several US, Canadian, and Japanese carriers lock phones that are purchased from them.

Does your smartphone or portable WiFi operate in Korea?
Your phone won't function if the local network is incompatible with it.

The two service providers in South Korea that supply tourist SIM cards are SK Telecom and KT Olleh, and they use the following network frequencies:

Bands 1 (2100 MHz), 3 (1800 MHz), 5 (850 MHz), and 8 of 4G LTE (900MHz)
HSDPA 2100MHz/HSDPA+ are 3G bands.

Verify that your phone can use these frequencies. The supported frequencies for your phone will be included in the technical specifications,

How to Examine a South Korean SIM card Before purchasing one

Of course, there are significant variances between the various SIM cards. What to look for while selecting your Korean SIM card is described below.

The SIM cards used by tourists are mostly exclusively Data or Data + Voice SIM cards.

Most guests won't need much more than this kind of SIM. You may still phone and text using Skype, WhatsApp, Google Hangouts, and other similar programs even when voice calls and text messaging are not supported.

You must choose a Data+Voice SIM if you do need a local phone number.

Duration

There is a maximum number of days that all prepaid SIM cards may be used. When you activate the SIM, this time period begins. While extensions are sometimes feasible, they are not always possible, so be sure to ask about them when ordering your SIM.

If extensions are not feasible, you can consider purchasing two cards. However, not all service providers let one individual buy several cards.

The longest possible rental length is 90 days. A resident card will be needed for longer stays.

Allowance for data

Despite the fact that many SIM cards provide limitless data, the fair use policy (FUP) differs greatly depending on the available alternatives. According to a fair use policy, the speed will be reduced if a certain quantity of data has been utilized in a specific length of time, often over the course of a day.

Some companies restrict the speed after 2 or 3 GB have been used in a single day. According to our observations, this is rather kind. 3 GB is equal to 36 hours of internet surfing, 600 hours of music streaming, or 6 hours of viewing a standard definition movie.

Others limit high-speed data use to 500 MB per day. This is enough if you just infrequently connect to the internet, but if you stream music or videos or often check your social media accounts, you will rapidly exceed the restrictions of this membership.

Once the data cap is reached, the speed is either 3G or 2G. If you're accustomed to 4G, the connection may be frustratingly slow but may be enough for checking out some basic websites.

The FUP may sometimes be raised by topping up the cards, although this is the exception rather than the norm.

Take up

While some SIM cards are mailed (for no charge), the majority of SIMs must be picked up at the airport.

Make sure to note or print the pickup location's address and its operating hours. (Until you pick up your SIM, you won't be able to access the internet.)

A little map indicating where to pick up your SIM may sometimes be included on the purchase page or in the confirmation email. Printing this map or storing it locally on your phone is an excellent idea since you won't have internet access until after you pick up your SIM.

Not every collection point is always open.Check ahead of time to see whether the place will be open when you arrive, and keep in mind that you'll need to clear immigration. It's also a good idea to leave yourself some breathing room in case your trip is delayed.

various-size SIM

A multi-size SIM's appearance

SIM card for Korea with airport pickup

Online pre-order for a Korea SIM card

Here is a list of the several prepaid Korean SIM cards that you may purchase in advance online. By provider, the overview is arranged.

The Benefits of Placing an Advance Purchase for Your Korean SIM card

If you have just returned from a long trip, you are undoubtedly sleepy and not in the ideal condition to decide which SIM you need.

You are advised to buy your South Korean SIM card in advance online and have it sent to your home address or available for pick-up at the airport.

Another benefit of placing an order online is that you have all the time you need to weigh your alternatives.

South Korea's Busan Skyline

Korea SIM cards with pick-up at Seoul and/or Busan airports (KT Olleh) (data or data + international calls and texts) provide views of Busan's spectacular skyline at night.

The biggest telephone provider in South Korea is called KT, or Korea Telecom. The brand name for cellphone broadband services is Olleh.

A prepaid SIM card that also permits outbound phone calls and text messaging is an option, as is a data-only SIM.

Where Pre-orders for KT SIM Cards May Be Made

GetYourGuide supports inbound calls, SMS messages, and data-only SIM cards. To make voice calls, the SIM may be topped up.

Klook: A prepaid or data-only SIM that enables phone and text

Data-only SIMs with top-up capabilities or preloaded SIMs are annoying (the prepaid SIM comes with a starting balance of KRW 11,000, enough for 42 minutes of domestic calls).

Incoming calls and text messages are supported by all SIMs, including data-only SIMs. These are never billed. The only card that doesn't have a local Korean number is the single-day card that may be obtained via Trazy.

All SIM cards support online recharge and extension. You must do this before they run out.

Size: SIM cards come in various sizes (normal, nano, and micro). Any mobile phone may use the SIM with little modification.

Channel: KT Olleh

Duration: 1 day, 5 days, 10 days, or 30 days (only available on Trazy).

Unfortunately, not all websites have every pickup option.

Check the pickup sites' hours carefully since many are not open around the clock.

You may choose between Seoul-Incheon airport terminals 1 and 2 when placing an order with Klook.

Gimpo, Incheon, Busan, and two places in the heart of Seoul are all available via GetYourGuide. (Myeong-dong and Hongdae)

You may choose to pick up the SIM at the airports of Incheon, Gimpo, or Busan while using Trazy. Additionally, they provide pick-up services at the Myeongdong and Hongik University subway stations.

At the counter, the SIM card will be activated. A refund will be issued if the SIM will not function for whatever reason. If you'd like, you may activate data-only SIM cards later. You must let the staff know at the time of pickup if you wish to activate your prepaid SIM at a later time.

Only required if you want to send texts or make phone calls.

The cost is $ GetYourGuide: only-data SIM (voice call top-ups are possible).

5 days: 35,700 KRW

10 days: 47,590 KRW

20 days: 74.787 KRW

90,079 KRW for 30 days

Verify costs and availability:

SIM Getyourguide

Klook: SIM-only for data (top-up for voice calls possible)

5 days: 24,400 KRW

10 days: 34,700 KRW

20 days: 60.500 KRW

30 days: 64,400 KRW

Verify costs and availability:

SIM Klook just for data

When placing an order, take care to choose the appropriate service type.

CONCLUSION

A. Recap of the Important Information: South Korea is a stunning and interesting nation that presents a rich cultural legacy, diversified natural beauty, and a wealth of adventure options. The ideal time to visit, the kind of lodging that best fits their requirements and budget, and the available local transit alternatives should all be considered when making a travel itinerary. Aside from learning about the health and safety concerns, they should also try the delectable Korean food, see the many landmarks and events, and experience the cuisine.

B. Vacation Tips for South Korea: Visitors will have a lifelong memory of South Korea since it is a unique and memorable travel location. Everyone may find something to enjoy in South Korea, regardless of their interests in nature, adventure, history, or culture. South Korea is a nation that genuinely needs to be experienced, from the pulsating metropolis of Seoul to the breathtaking natural scenery of Jeju Island. South Korea is a place that every visitor should put on their bucket list because of its kind and hospitable people, delectable cuisine, and variety of activities.

Printed in Great Britain
by Amazon

18650192R00068